At Issue

How Does Advertising Impact Teen Behavior?

Other Books in the At Issue Series:

At Issue

How Does Advertising Impact Teen Behavior?

David M. Haugen, Book Editor

GREENHAVEN PRESS
A part of Gale, Cengage Learning

GALE
CENGAGE Learning

Detroit • New York • San Francisco • New Haven, Conn • Waterville, Maine • London

GALE
CENGAGE Learning™

Christine Nasso, *Publisher*
Elizabeth Des Chenes, *Managing Editor*

© 2008 Greenhaven Press, a part of Gale, Cengage Learning.

Gale and Greenhaven Press are registered trademarks used herein under license.

For more information, contact:
Greenhaven Press
27500 Drake Rd.
Farmington Hills, MI 48331-3535
Or you can visit our Internet site at gale.cengage.com

For product information and technology assistance, contact us at

Gale Customer Support, 1-800-877-4253
For permission to use material from this text or product, submit all requests online at
www.cengage.com/permissions

Further permissions questions can be emailed to permissionrequest@cengage.com

Articles in Greenhaven Press anthologies are often edited for length to meet page requirements. In addition, original titles of these works are changed to clearly present the main thesis and to explicitly indicate the author's opinion. Every effort is made to ensure that Greenhaven Press accurately reflects the original intent of the authors. Every effort has been made to trace the owners of copyrighted material.

Cover photograph reproduced by permission of Images.com/Corbis.

LIBRARY OF CONGRESS CATALOGING-IN-PUBLICATION DATA

How does advertising impact teen behavior? / David M. Haugen, book editor.
    p. cm. -- (At issue)
Includes bibliographical references and index.
ISBN-13: 978-0-7377-3922-0 (hardcover)
ISBN-13: 978-0-7377-3923-7 (pbk.)
1. Mass media and teenagers. 2. Advertising. 3. Teenagers--Attitudes. 4. Behavioral assessment of teenagers. 5. Criminal liability--United States. I. Haugen, David M., 1969-
    HQ799.2.M35H38 2008
    659.10835--dc22

                                                                    2007048660

Printed in the United States of America
    1 2 3 4 5   13 12 11 10 09
ED071

Contents

Introduction

The American Academy of Pediatrics reported in June 2007 that American teenagers spend $155 billion a year on consumer goods. Their younger brothers and sisters spend up to $25 billion, and together they influence another $200 billion of their parents' spending. Marketing executives are eager to tap into this abundant cash flow. They have directed much of their advertising spending toward teenage consumers, especially, hawking their brands between the pages of teen magazines, in commercials during teens' favorite television programs, and even on the walls of their bathroom stalls at school. One growing marketing trend is advertising on the Internet, a venue where merchandisers know they are sure to reach teenagers around the clock.

In an effort to connect with teenage consumers on the World Wide Web, some corporations are developing social networking forums in which to advertise their products. The Wendy's corporation, for example, has created a networking page for its cartoon hamburger mascot called Smart on the trendy MySpace.com site. More than eighty-one thousand Internet users have joined Smart's social network and are capable of viewing the mascot's personal profile. Also, as Laura Petrecca reports for *USA Today*, the burger pal enjoys metal music, Angelina Jolie, and the hit television show *24*—all, coincidentally, teen favorites.

MySpace.com is one of the best-known networking sites on the Web, drawing more than 46 million visitors each month, according to Nielsen/NetRatings. In addition to Wendy's, other marketers have taken advantage of advertising to the MySpace.com audience. The Burger King king has a MySpace page, and as Petrecca reports, even fictional characters from movies and television programs are sporting their own profiles on the site. For example, Columbia Pictures posted a profile for actor Will Ferrell's racecar driving character Ricky Bobby from *Talladega Nights*. The FX cable channel also created a profile for its serial killer character, The Carver, from the hit drama *Nip/Tuck*.

While teen Internet users may enjoy the corporate-sponsored profiles on MySpace.com, many may not recognize these networking pages as the advertising they are. Michael Berrett is the chief revenue officer at Fox Interactive Media, the group that sells advertising space on MySpace. He tells *USA Today* that marketers spend from $100,000 to $1 million for banner ads and profile promotion on MySpace.com. Petrecca notes that in addition to reaching millions of Internet users through the site, MySpace.com also offers to monitor profile pages for its corporate advertisers, removing negative postings about products from the networking site upon request.

Max Kalehoff is the vice president of marketing at Nielsen BuzzMetrics, which monitors consumer-generated postings on the Web. He has insight into the possible negative ramifications of selling too much advertising space on social networking sites. As he tells Petrecca, "There's a ton of advertising dollars that are waiting to throw themselves into these platforms, but ultimately, the value comes from the members. What draws members into these gathering places is the realness and authenticity. . . . The bombardment of commercialism could destroy what makes it great in the first place."

Wendy's, for one, seems to value this atmosphere of authenticity that sites such as MySpace are trying to create. Its chief marketing officer Ian Rowden tells Petrecca that the corporation has chosen not to have MySpace advertising monitors remove negative postings that may appear on Smart's profile page. "It's a social dialogue," he says. "If we took the posts down, it would send a message that's not consistent with the character" of the site. So far, it seems that MySpace.com's young adult audience is open to corporate use of the site as long as the profiles are entertaining and engaging, Petrecca reports. As twenty-year-old Eliza Madison of New York tells her, corporate marketing is a "good way of using the network if [advertisers] make [the profiles] funny and people enjoy it. But they have to do it in a way that doesn't make you feel like you're being attacked by the company to go out and buy their stuff."

One company that just might not make the cut with today's advertising savvy teens on the Web is Wal-Mart. In June 2006, the corporate giant announced its plans to create its own MySpace-like networking site at walmart.com/ schoolyourway. The site encourages teens to create their own profile page for a chance to have their videos chosen for Wal-Mart television commercials. Unlike MySpace, however, Wal-Mart executives maintain tight restrictions on their site. As Mya Frazier reports in the June 2006 issue of *Advertising Age*, profile page content on the Wal-Mart site is limited to a headline, a fashion quiz, and a favorite song. Wal-Mart also reserves the right to edit all video content for objectionable material.

While Wal-Mart encourages teens visiting its site to express their individuality, Frazier writes that the company not only "screens all content," but also, "tells parents their kids have joined and forbids users to email one another," two decidedly "uncool" features for a site that is striving to be hip. Fourteen-year-old Amy Kandel from Ohio agrees that Wal-Mart has missed the mark with its social networking efforts. As she reports to Frazier, the teens on the site's opening pages do not look like "real" kids. Instead, they "looked like they were trying to be supercool, but they weren't at all, and they were just being kind of weird." Eighteen-year-old Pete Hughes adds, "It just seemed kind of corny to me."

Tim Stock, with New York's Scenario DNA, a research firm devoted to studying Generation Y, thinks Wal-Mart's tight controls over the site are, as Frazier writes, "cementing the retailer's image as a conformist brand." He adds, "The second you try to create boundaries and draw a line around content and put a box around content, it becomes something else. Teens aren't searching for what a company deems relevant, but what they deem relevant. You can't own it. When anyone tries to own it too much, then it becomes a problem. That's the impression I get on this site."

Regardless of Wal-Mart's seeming failure on the social networking scene, other corporations are bound to continue to strive for successful advertising campaigns in this venue online. As more teens embrace the increasing capabilities of cell phone technology, marketers are, likewise, embracing new opportunities to reach them on their cells as well. According to Louise Story of the *New York Times*, Coca-Cola introduced Sprite Yard to cell phone users in China in June 2007. Like MySpace online, Sprite Yard allows consumers to set up personal profiles, swap photos, and chat online via their cell phones, rather than their computers. The success of Sprite Yard has yet to be determined, but its existence proves one thing for sure: wherever teens roam—on the Web or on the go—advertisers will surely follow.

1

Teens Encounter Advertising from a Variety of Sources

American Academy of Pediatrics

The American Academy of Pediatrics is an organization of sixty thousand pediatricians committed to the attainment of optimal physical, mental, and social health and well-being for all infants, children, adolescents, and young adults.

Young people in America are bombarded by advertising every day. Marketers reach them through commercials on television and also through ads in magazines, on billboards, on the Internet, and even in the bathroom stalls at school. Much advertising has a negative effect on teens, encouraging them to drink alcohol, smoke cigarettes, and look favorably upon unnecessary prescription drugs to cure all that ails them. Advertisements for food and restaurants also impact teens, causing them to choose high-calorie, non-nutritious foods over healthful ones. Some of this negative impact from advertising could be prevented, however, by teaching teens about the effects of advertising.

Several European countries forbid or severely curtail advertising to children; in the United States, on the other hand, selling to children is simply "business as usual." The average young person views more than 3000 ads per day on television (TV), on the Internet, on billboards, and in magazines. Increasingly, advertisers are targeting younger and younger children in an effort to establish "brand-name preference" at as

American Academy of Pediatrics, "Children, Adolescents, and Advertising," *Pediatrics*, vol. 118, December 6, 2006, p. 2563–2566. Copyright © 2006 American Academy of Pediatrics. Used with permission. http://pediatrics.aappublications.org/cgi/content/full/ 118/6/2563.

early an age as possible. This targeting occurs because advertising is a $250 billion/year industry with 900,000 brands to sell, and children and adolescents are attractive consumers: teenagers spend $155 billion/year, children younger than 12 years spend another $25 billion, and both groups influence perhaps another $200 billion of their parents' spending per year Increasingly, advertisers are seeking to find new and creative ways of targeting young consumers via the Internet, in schools, and even in bathroom stalls.

The Effects of Advertising on Children and Adolescents

Research has shown that young children—younger than 8 years—are cognitively and psychologically defenseless against advertising. They do not understand the notion of intent to sell and frequently accept advertising claims at face value. In fact, in the late 1970s, the Federal Trade Commission (FTC) held hearings, reviewed the existing research, and came to the conclusion that it was unfair and deceptive to advertise to children younger than 6 years. What kept the FTC from banning such ads was that it was thought to be impractical to implement such a ban. However, some Western countries have done exactly that: Sweden and Norway forbid all advertising directed at children younger than 12 years, Greece bans toy advertising until after 10 PM, and Denmark and Belgium severely restrict advertising aimed at children.

Advertising in Different Media

Television Children and adolescents view 40,000 ads per year on TV alone. This occurs despite the fact that the Children's Television Act of 1990 (Pub L No. 101-437) limits advertising on children's programming to 10.5 minutes/hour on weekends and 12 minutes/hour on weekdays. However, much of children's viewing occurs during prime time, which features nearly 16 minutes/hour of advertising. A 30-second ad during the Super Bowl now costs $2.3 million but reaches 80 million people.

Movies A 2000 FTC investigation found that violent movies, music, and video games have been intentionally marketed to children and adolescents. Although movie theaters have agreed not to show trailers for R-rated movies before G-rated movies in response to the release of the FTC report, children continue to see advertising for violent media in other venues. For instance, M-rated video games, which according to the gaming industry's own rating system are not recommended for children younger than 17 years, are frequently advertised in movie theaters, video game magazines, and publications with high youth readership. Also, movies targeted at children often prominently feature brand-name products and fast food restaurants. In 1997-1998, 8 alcohol companies placed products in 233 motion pictures and in 1 episode or more of 181 TV series.

Print Media According to the Consumer's Union, more than 160 magazines are now targeted at children. Young people see 45% more beer ads and 27% more ads for hard liquor in teen magazines than adults do in their magazines. Despite the Master Settlement Agreement with the tobacco industry in 1998, tobacco advertising expenditures in 38 youth-oriented magazines amounted to $217 million in 2000.

The Internet An increasing number of Web sites try to entice children and teenagers to make direct sales. Teenagers account for more than $1 billion in e-commerce dollars, and the industry spent $21.6 million on Internet banner ads alone in 2002. More than 100 commercial Web sites promote alcohol products. The content of these sites varies widely, from little more than basic brand information to chat rooms, "virtual bars," drink recipes, games, contests, and merchandise catalogues. Many of these sites use slick promotional techniques to target young people. In 1998, the Children's Online Privacy Protection Act (Pub I, No. 105-277) was passed, which mandates that commercial Web sites cannot knowingly collect information from children younger than 13 years. These sites are required to provide notice on the site to parents about their collection, use, and disclosure of children's personal information and must obtain "verifiable parental consent" before collecting, using, or disclosing this information.

Advertisers have traditionally used techniques to which children and adolescents are more susceptible, such as product placements in movies and TV shows.

Marketing Techniques

Advertisers have traditionally used techniques to which children and adolescents are more susceptible, such as product placements in movies and TV shows, tie-ins between movies and fast food restaurants, tie-ins between TV shows and toy action figures or other products kids' clubs that are linked to popular shows, and celebrity endorsements. Cellular phones are currently being marketed to 6- to 12-year-olds, with the potential for directing specific advertisers to children and pre-teens. Coca-Cola reportedly paid Warner Bros. Studios $150 million for the global marketing rights to the movie "Harry Potter and the Sorcerer's Stone," and nearly 20% of fast food restaurant ads now mention a toy premium in their ads. Certain tie-in products may be inappropriate for children (eg, action figures from the World Wrestling Federation or an action doll that mutters profanities from an R-rated *Austin Powers* movie).

Children's advertising protections will need to be updated for digital TV, which will be in place before 2010. In the near future, children watching a TV program will be able to click an on-screen link and go to a Web site during the program.

Interactive games and promotions on digital TV will have the ability to lure children away from regular programming, encouraging them to spend a long time in an environment that lacks clear separation between content and advertising. Interactive technology may also allow advertisers to collect vast amounts of information about children's viewing habits and preferences and target them on the basis of that information.

Specific Health-related Areas of Concern

Tobacco Advertising Tobacco manufacturers spend $30 million/day ($11.2 billion/year) on advertising and promotion. Exposure to tobacco advertising may be a bigger risk factor than having family members and peers who smoke and can even undermine the effect of strong parenting practices. Two unique and large longitudinal studies have found that approximately one third of all adolescent smoking can be attributed to tobacco advertising and promotions. In addition, more than 20 studies have found that children exposed to cigarette ads or promotions are more likely to become smokers themselves. Recent evidence has emerged that tobacco companies have specifically targeted teenagers as young as 13 years of age.

Alcohol Advertising Alcohol manufacturers spend $5.7 billion/year on advertising and promotion. Young people typically view 2000 beer and wine commercials annually, with most of the ads concentrated in sports programming. During prime time, only 1 alcohol ad appears every 4 hours; yet, in sports programming, the frequency increases to 2.4 ads per hour. Research has found that adolescent drinkers are more likely to have been exposed to alcohol advertising. Given that children begin making decisions about alcohol at an early age—probably during grade school—exposure to beer commercials represents a significant risk factor. Minority children may be at particular risk.

Drug Advertising "Just Say No" as a message to teenagers about drugs seems doomed to failure given that $11 billion/year is spent on cigarette advertising, $5.7 billion/year is spent on alcohol advertising, and nearly $4 billion/year is spent on prescription drug advertising. Drug companies now spend more than twice as much on marketing as they do on research and development. The top 10 drug companies made a total profit of $35.9 billion in 2002—more than the other 490 companies in the Fortune 500 combined. Is such advertising effective? A recent survey of physicians found that 92% of patients had requested an advertised drug. In addition, children and teenagers may get the message that there is a drug available to cure all ills and heal all pain, a drug for every occasion (including sexual intercourse).

Food Advertising and Obesity Advertisers spend more than $2.5 billion/year to promote restaurants and another $2 billion to promote food products. On TV, of the estimated 40,000 ads per year that young people see, half are for food, especially sugared cereals and high-calorie snacks. Healthy foods are advertised less than 3% of the time; children rarely see a food advertisement for broccoli. Increasingly, fast food conglomerates are using toy tie-ins with major children's motion pictures to try to attract young people. Nearly 20% of fast food ads now mention a toy premium in their commercials. Several studies document that young children request more junk food (defined as foods with high-calorie density but very low nutrient density) after viewing commercials. In 1 study, the amount of TV viewed per week correlated with requests for specific foods and with caloric intake. At the same time, advertising healthy foods has been shown to increase wholesome eating in children as young as 3 to 6 years of age.

Sex in Advertising Sex is used in commercials to sell everything from beer to shampoo to cars. New research is showing that teenagers' exposure to sexual content in the media may be responsible for earlier onset of sexual intercourse or other sexual activities. What is increasingly apparent is the discrepancy between the abundance of advertising of products for erectile dysfunction (ED) (between January and October, 2004, drug companies spent $343 million advertising Viagra, Levitra, and Cialis) and the lack of advertising for birth control products or emergency contraceptives on the major TV networks. This is despite the fact that 2 national polls have found that a majority of Americans favor the advertising of birth control on TV. Ads for ED drugs give children and teens inappropriate messages about sex and sexuality at a time when they are not being taught well in school sex education programs. Research has definitively found that giving teenagers increased access to birth control through advertising does not make them sexually active at a younger age.

American advertising also frequently uses female models who are anorectic in appearance and, thus, may contribute to the development of a distorted body self-image and abnormal eating behaviors in young girls.

Advertisers have slowly but steadily infiltrated school systems around the country.

Advertising in Schools

Advertisers have slowly but steadily infiltrated school systems around the country. The "3 Rs" have now become the "4 Rs," with the fourth R being "retail." Ads are now appearing on school buses, in gymnasiums, on book covers, and even in bathroom stalls. More than 200 school districts nationwide have signed exclusive contracts with soft drink companies. These agreements specify the number and placement of soda-vending machines, which is ironic given that schools risk losing federal subsidies for their free breakfast and lunch programs if they serve soda in their cafeterias. In addition, there are more than 4500 Pizza Hut chains and 3000 Taco Bell chains in school cafeterias around the country.

There is some good news, however. In May, 2006, the nation's largest beverage distributors agreed to halt nearly all sales of sodas to public schools and sell only water, unsweetened juice, and low-fat milk in elementary and middle schools. Diet sodas would be sold only in high schools.

School advertising also appears under the guise of educational TV: Channel One. Currently available in 12,000 schools, Channel One consists of 10 minutes of current-events programming and 2 minutes of commercials. Advertisers pay $200,000 for advertising time and the opportunity to target 40% of the nation's teenagers for 30 seconds. According to a recent government report, Channel One now plays in 25% of the nation's middle and high schools and generates profits estimated at $100 million annually.

Conclusions

Clearly, advertising represents "big business" in the United States and can have a significant effect on young people. Unlike free speech, commercial speech does not enjoy the same protections under the First Amendment of the Constitution. Advertisements can be restricted or even banned if there is a significant public health risk. Cigarette advertising and alcohol advertising would seem to fall squarely into this category, and ads for junk food could easily be restricted.

One solution that is noncontroversial and would be easy to implement is to educate children and teenagers about the effects of advertising—media literacy. Curricula have been developed that teach young people to become critical viewers of media in all of its forms, including advertising. Media education seems to be protective in mitigating harmful effects of media, including the effects of cigarette, alcohol, and food advertising.

2

Advertisers View Teens as Marketing Opportunities

Mary Story and Simone French

Mary Story, PhD, RD, and Simone French, PhD are faculty in the Division of Epidemiology at the University of Minnesota in Minneapolis. Professor Story is director of the Robert Wood Foundation Healthy Eating Research Program, National Program Office, and co-director of the Obesity Prevention Center. Professor French is co-director of the Obesity Prevention Center and member of the University of Minnesota Cancer Center.

Young people in America are bombarded with advertising every day. Marketers reach them through commercials on television and also through ads in magazines, on billboards, on the Internet and even in the bathroom stalls at school. Much advertising has a negative effect on adolescents, encouraging them to adopt unhealthy behaviors. Advertising for food and restaurants impacts children and teens, causing them to choose high-calorie, non-nutritious foods over healthy ones.

Numerous studies have documented that young children have little understanding of the persuasive intent of advertising. Prior to age 7 or 8 years, children tend to view advertising as fun, entertaining, and unbiased information. An understanding of advertising intent usually develops by the time most children are 7–8 years old. Because of their level of cognitive development, children under 8 years of age are

Mary Story and Simone French, *International Journal of Behavioral Nutrition and Physical Activity*, London, BioMed Central, 2004. Copyright © 2004 Story and French, licensee BioMed Central Ltd. Reproduced by permission. http://www/ijbnpa.org/content/ 1/1/3.

viewed by many child development researchers as a population vulnerable to misleading advertising. The heavy marketing of high fat, high sugar foods to this age group can be viewed as exploitative because young children do not understand that commercials are designed to sell products and they do not yet possess the cognitive ability to comprehend or evaluate the advertising. Preteens, from ages 8–10 years, possess the cognitive ability to process advertisements but do not necessarily do so. From early adolescence (11–12 years), children's thinking becomes more multidimensional, involving abstract as well as concrete thought. Adolescents still can be persuaded by the emotive messages of advertising, which play into their developmental concerns related to appearance, self-identity, belonging, and sexuality.

Food Advertising and Marketing Channels

Multiple channels are used to reach youth to foster brand-building and influence food product purchase behavior. Youth-oriented marketing channels and techniques include television advertising, in-school marketing, product placements, kids clubs, the Internet, toys and products with brand logos, and youth-targeted promotions, such as cross-selling and tie-ins. The channels used to market food and beverages to youth are described below.

By the time they graduate from high school [children in the United States] may have been exposed to 360,000 television ads.

Television Advertising

It is estimated that US children may view between 20,000–40,000 commercials each year and by the time they graduate from high school may have been exposed to 360,000 television ads. Food is the most frequently advertised product category on US children's television and food ads account for over 50% of all ads targeting children. Children view an average of one food commercial every five minutes of television viewing time, and may see as many as three hours of food commercials each week. In a descriptive study that examined US food advertising during 52.5 hours of Saturday morning children's programming, 564 food advertisements (57% of all ads) were shown. On average, 11 of 19 commercials per hour were for food. Of these ads, 246 (44%) promoted food from the fats and sweets group, such as candy, soft drinks, chips, cakes, cookies and pastries. Fast-food restaurant advertising was also prevalent, comprising 11% of total food advertisements. The most frequently advertised food product was high sugar breakfast cereal. There were no advertisements for fruits or vegetables. Several other studies have documented that the foods promoted on US children's television are predominantly high in sugar and fat, with almost no references to fruits or vegetables. The food advertised on US children's television programming is inconsistent with healthy eating recommendations for children.

In-school Marketing

During the past decade in the US, use of public schools as advertising and marketing venues has grown. Reasons for the increase in in-school marketing to children and adolescents include the desire to increase sales and generate product loyalty, the ability to reach large numbers of children and adolescents in a contained setting, and the financial vulnerability of schools due to chronic funding shortages. In-school commercial activities related to food and beverages include 1) product sales; 2) direct advertising; 3) indirect advertising; and 4) market research with students.

In a recent report by the US General Accounting Office (GAO), food sales were reported to be the most prevalent form of commercial activity in schools. Food sales involved primarily the sale of soft drinks from vending machines and short-term fundraising sales. The US national School Health Policies and Programs Study 2000 (SHPPS) found that students could purchase soft drinks, sports drinks, or fruit drinks that are not 100% juice in a vending machine, school store, or snack bar in 58% of elementary schools, 83% of middle schools, and 94% of high schools. In a recent survey of 336 secondary school principals in Minnesota, US, 98% of the school principals reported that soft drink vending machines were available to students, and 77% of the schools had a contract with a soft drink company. The GAO report found that the sale of soft drinks by schools or districts under exclusive contracts is the fastest growing activity of all product sales. Nationally in the US, more than one-third of elementary schools, half of middle/junior high schools, and almost three-fourths of senior high schools have a contract that gives a company rights to sell soft drinks at schools. Most (92%) of these schools receive a specified percentage of the soft drink sales revenues and about 40% receive incentives such as cash awards or donated equipment once revenues total a specified amount. The contract terms vary greatly, but many are highly lucrative.

There is also a growing trend of fast food vendors in schools. About 20% of US high schools offer brand-name fast foods, such as Pizza Hut, Taco Bell, or Subway. The results from the 2000 California High School Fast Food Survey conducted in 171 US school districts with 345 public high schools found that 24% of districts with a fast food or beverage contract gave exclusive advertising promotion rights to that company, including placement of the company's name and logo on school equipment and facilities. Only 13% of the districts did not allow advertising on campus.

There are many types of direct advertising in schools, such as soft drink, fast food, or snack food corporate logos on athletic scoreboards, sponsorship banners in gyms, ads in school newspapers and yearbooks, free textbook covers with ads, and screen-saver ads on school computers for branded foods and beverages. The US GAO report found that the most visible and prevalent types of direct advertising in schools were soft drink advertisements and corporate names and logos on scoreboards. Recently, food marketing to youth in schools has become even more intense, persuasive, and creative. Some schools are now selling food advertising space on their athletes' warm-up suits, as well as inside and outside of school buses.

Food advertisements can also be delivered through in-school media. About 12,000 schools or about 38% of middle and high schools in the US are connected to Channel One, the 12-minute current events program that carries two minutes of commercials including advertisements for soft drinks and high fat snack foods. Schools receive free video equipment in exchange for mandatory showing of the program in classrooms. Brand and Greenberg evaluated the effects of Channel One in-school advertising on high school students' purchasing attitudes, intentions, and behaviors. About 70% of the 45 food commercials shown on Channel One during one month were for food products including fast foods, soft dunks, chips and candy. In schools where Channel One was viewed, students had more positive attitudes about the advertised products, and were more likely to report intentions to purchase these products compared to students who did not have Channel One in their classrooms. However, students who watched Channel One did not report more frequent purchases of the advertised products compared with students in schools that did not show Channel One.

In the last 10 years, US marketing companies have developed strategies that focus exclusively on schools. For example, a US marketing company, Cover Concepts, distributes textbook covers, lesson plans, posters, bookmarks, sampling programs, specialty packs, and lunch menu posters to participating companies. These products are branded with the company's name or corporate logo and then distributed free to students and schools. Cover Concepts' promotional materials state: "Cover Concepts places your brand directly into the hands of kids and teens in a clutter-free environment. We work in tandem with school administrators to distribute free, advertiser-sponsored materials to over 30 million student—grades K-12—in 43,000 authorized schools nationwide, plus additional reach in daycare centers throughout the country."

Indirect advertising includes corporate-sponsored educational materials and corporate-sponsored incentives and contests.

Product Placements

Product placement is increasing in popularity and becoming more acceptable as a standard marketing channel. It typically involves incorporating brands in movies in return for money or promotional support. Fees are variable depending on the relative prominence of the placement in movies, and are usually around $50,000 to $100,000. The product placement may be placed as a backdrop "prop" or may be an integral part of the script. Producers contend that product placement makes sets look more realistic and that brands help define characters and settings. In addition, product placement can help offset production costs. Product placement in the movies first gained attention in 1982 when it was reported that sales of the peanut butter candy Hershey's Reese's Pieces increased by 65% within a month due to its placement within *E.T., The Extra Terrestrial*. It is reported that placement is being used more in radio, music videos, books, comic strips, plays, and songs and that product placement agencies are increasing in number.

Kids' Club

Several corporations have developed branded kids clubs as a way to communicate with and maintain an ongoing relationship with children. The name is a misnomer in that many kids clubs aren't really clubs, but standard marketing programs with names that imply they are clubs. Kids clubs permit mass marketing on a personalized basis and club members may receive direct mailing such as membership cards, birthday cards, holiday greetings, and newsletters. In addition they can participate in contests, receive coupons and branded items such as posters, screensavers, and discounts for items with the club's logo. Some examples of kids clubs from corporations include Burger King, Nickelodeon, Fox, Sega, and Disney. The Burger King Kids Club has more than 5 million members.

Internet

Online media play an increasingly significant role in the lives of US children and teenagers. US Census data indicate that between 1998 and 2001 the proportion of US adolescents (ages 14–17 years) using the Internet increased from 51% to 75% and the proportion of US children (ages 10–13 years) online increased from 39% to 65%. Families with children represent one of the fastest growing segments of the population using the Internet. US Census data from 2001 indicate that half (51%) of US children 10–13 years old and 61% of those 14–17 years old have Internet access at home.

Advertisers and marketers have begun to target the rapidly growing number of U.S. children online with a variety of new interactive advertising and marketing techniques.

Advertisers and marketers have begun to target the rapidly growing number of US children online with a variety of new interactive advertising and marketing techniques. The forms of advertising and marketing on the Web differ significantly from television commercials. Utilizing the unique features of the Internet, companies can seamlessly integrate advertising and Web site content. Almost all of the major companies that advertise and market to children have created their own websites, designed as "branded environments" for children. This electronic advertising "environment" and on-line infomercials is evident with food companies, which offer multiple entertaining, animated and interactive areas developed specifically for preschoolers and children around their food products. These sites include games, word-find puzzles, contests, quizzes, riddles, music, e-mail cards, clips of commercials, sweepstakes, downloadable recipes, desktop wallpaper and screensavers that feature their products, and on-line stores that sell licensed merchandise. Children can also sign up to receive electronic newsletters with news about products and promotions. The sites often feature popular product spokescharacters and animated cartoon characters, such as Tony the Tiger, Chester Cheetah, Toucan Sam, and Snap! Crackle! And Pop! The integration of products into games is commonplace. The company's website is frequently featured on ads or product packaging.

Youth-targeted Promotions

Promotions are a commonly used marketing method for reaching children and adolescents and include cross-selling, tie-ins, premiums, and sweepstakes prizes. Cross-selling and tie-ins combine promotional efforts to sell a product. In the US, the food industry has forged promotional links with Hollywood and Network studios, toy companies, and sports leagues. Burger King has formed a linkage with Nickelodeon, and McDonald's with the Fox Kids Network. Burger King has sold chicken nuggets shaped like Teletubbies. Disney has launched cross-selling campaigns and tie-ins worth millions of dollars to promote its films and characters. In 1996, Disney signed a ten-year global marketing agreement with McDonald's. In 2001, Coca-Cola and Disney partnered to build Disney character-branded children's beverages. Kellogg's also has an agreement with Disney to extend the Disney characters to cereals, Keebler cookies and Eggo waffles. McDonald's has formed partnerships with the National Basketball Association. Pizza Hut, Taco Bell and Wendy's have linked with the National Collegiate Athletic Association.

Premiums and sweepstakes prizes have increased recently and are often used to appeal to children's and adolescent's tastes and desires. Premiums provide something free with a purchase, whereas sweepstakes and contests promise opportunities to win free products. Fast food restaurants typically use premiums in children's meals, giving away simple toys. Sweetened cereals also commonly give premiums in the form of toys, cards or games. Premiums can increase short-term sales since children may desire the item over the food, but they also can help elevate the image of that brand in children's minds. In one study in which preschool and school-age children and parents were unobtrusively observed while grocery shopping, almost half of the children who made cereal purchase requests were influenced by premium offers.

3

Brands, Not Marketers, Define Teens

Deanna Zammit

Deanna Zammit is a frequent contributor to Adweek.

Today's teens do not allow brands to define them, but they do use brand names as a means to express themselves. They like to feel as though they are discovering trends on their own rather than being pushed into brands by merchandisers. Advertisers are turning to guerilla marketing techniques to reach teens who have become cynical about advertising, making contact through cell phone text messaging and Web sites.

Jocks. Cheerleaders. Stoners. Skinheads. Gangsters. To the marketers trying to reach them, that roster may sound more like the cast in a John Hughes movie or the roll call of Ferris Bueller's fan club. But at *Adweek*'s What Teens Want conference held July 12, 2005 at the Marriott Marquis in New York, speakers made it clear that if marketers aren't thinking about how teens identify themselves within their peer set, their brands are going to miss the mark.

"There is no such thing as hitting teens [as a broad demographic]," said Malcolm Bird, svp [senior vice president] of AOL Kids and Teens, who spoke as part of a panel on targeting teens in an online and mobile world. "You've got to decide what sort of teens and what demo you want to hit within the media."

Today's teens think of brand names less as a hallmark of quality and more as a means of defining themselves.

"The brands allow them to express themselves politically," said Jim Taylor, vice chairman of The Harrison Group in Waterbury, Conn. "As individuals with a specific affinity for a style, as a badge of leadership."

Taylor, who surveyed more than 3,000 13- to 24-year-olds for a study entitled "Worlds of Possibility," grouped teens into five categories. A-Listers, typically referred to as the popular kids or the in-crowd, are star athletes and honor-roll students. American Dreamers were characterized as regular, hard-working teens. Individual Thinkers are opinionated, intolerant but leaders. Outsiders feel estranged and suffer from low self-esteem. And JBs, short for Jack Blacks, are party kids who are less career oriented than their peers.

Taylor said the common thread is "almost all of these kids believe they are someone else's leader." And that, marketers agreed, is where they need to come in. Advertising to teens cynical about marketing demands that kids believe they are "discovering" brands on their own.

[One marketer] uses an extensive network of teen influencers who are rewarded for promoting brands to their friends and acquaintances.

"They don't want to be told or pushed, they want to discover it for themselves," said Charlie Walk, an evp [executive vice president] at Columbia Records. Rather than a broad-based campaign for new artist Teddy Geiger, Walk said the company would seed his music among teen influencers through giveaways and free performances. When word-of-mouth crescendos in teen chat rooms, Columbia will promote the record on a wider basis, Walk said.

Guerilla Marketing

Carlos Scott vp [vice president] of marketing and corporate partnerships for guerilla marketing firm N-Vision hooked up R&B singer Jarvis with OT Overtime, a deodorant for tween boys that was placed in music videos and mentioned in performances. Ron Vos, founder of Hi Frequency Marketing, uses an extensive network of teen influencers who are rewarded for promoting brands to their friends and acquaintances. Both were members of the conference's Grass-Roots and Guerilla Marketing panel.

Still others are firm believers in creating online branded content for teens or reaching young buyers through their cell phones. Rich Nelson, president of Trendum USA, advocated staying abreast of text messaging slang and codes so that text messaged ads seem more authentic. Bird, of AOL Kids and Teens, suggested creating more than five 15-second executions for ads that air when teens log onto sites or download content, because they visit their favorite sites several times a day.

"This is the first generation that is going to adopt content generation on their mobiles," said Bird, in addition to buying ring tones. Web-enabled phones will make it possible to watch video clips and shop via cell phone, members of the online marketing panel said.

But for all the studies and speculation, members of the teen panel said TV, magazine and outdoor ads were most likely to influence their purchasing, and those methods continue to pose rudimentary challenges. Said one 16-year-old, "I like the Vonage ad where the guy is running on the treadmill and falls down. It's funny, but I still don't know what Vonage is."

4

Advertisers Seek Early Brand Loyalty from Youths

Julie Bosman

Julie Bosman is a former reporter and researcher for the New Republic *magazine and currently is a writer for the* New York Times.

In an effort to gain early brand loyalty from eight- to fifteen-year-olds, Toyota is marketing its Scion model in an interactive online community at Whyville.net. Here, gamers can purchase a virtual Scion, cruise the Internet landscape, and interact with other online visitors. Toyota hopes that kids visiting the site today will grow up to purchase a Toyota in the future. Until then, they might also have a significant impact on influencing their parents' car purchases.

In April 2006, Toyota quietly began an unusual virtual promotion of its small, boxy Scion: it paid for the car's product placement in Whyville.net, an online interactive community populated almost entirely by 8- to 15-year-olds.

Never mind that they cannot actually buy the car. Toyota is counting on Whyvillians to do two things—influence their parents' car purchases and maybe grow up with some Toyota brand loyalty.

It may appear counterintuitive, but Toyota says the promotion is working. Ten days into the campaign, visitors to the site had used the word "Scion" in online chats more than 78,000 times; hundreds of virtual Scions were purchased, using "clams," the currency of Whyville; and the community meeting place "Club Scion" was visited 33,741 times. These online Scion owners customized their cars, drove around the virtual Whyville and picked up their Scion-less friends for a ride.

Toyota is not the first car company to engage video game and online game audiences through product placement. Car companies like DaimlerChrysler have long pitched teenagers and young adults through product placements in video games, and Cadillac has incorporated its cars in a Microsoft Xbox 360 game.

Whyville was founded in 1999 as an educational online community and now reaches an audience of 1.6 million, who create their own personas within the site and interact with other visitors. The executives behind Whyville acknowledged the paradox of marketing a car to future drivers. "It's not lost on us, and it's not lost on Scion," said Jay Goss, the chief operating officer for Whyville. "By definition, this is a sponsor of Whyville that can't have as its customers the kids who visit the site. But they know that kids influence parents, and kids grow up."

Toyota is paying Whyville by the number of visitors on the site, but declined to name a figure.

Targeting so-called tweens or teenagers long before they can buy a product is a tactic that more marketers are exploring.

Early Branding

Targeting so-called tweens or teenagers long before they can buy a product is a tactic that more marketers are exploring, said Matthew Diamond, the chief executive of Alloy Media and Marketing, a consultancy in New York that specializes in youth marketing.

"It's early branding," Mr. Diamond said. "You are branding your product at a relevant time to the young person. You're establishing that brand presence and positive association, since important buying decisions are forthcoming."

For example, retailers like Staples and Office Depot are pitching high school juniors and seniors about products that they will buy in college, Mr. Diamond said. "They will begin to target you because they know you're going to be on your own," he said.

Since the Scion was introduced nationally [in 2004], Toyota has aggressively marketed it to young drivers. Its median buyer is 31, the youngest in the automotive industry, Toyota says. The company has employed nontraditional advertising strategies. For example, it sponsors monthly nightclub events and sells Scion-themed gear on its Web site, including D.J. bags ($55) and snowboard jackets ($180).

The power of younger consumers has grown stronger in recent years.

One of the goals in introducing the Scion was to cultivate an un-Toyota audience. Nearly 80 percent of Scion buyers are new to the Toyota family, said Deborah Senior, the national marketing and communications manager for Scion. In aiming at an underage audience, she said, the company is thinking about relationships with future car buyers. "I understand that they are very influential," Ms. Senior said of the intended audience. "The main goal is to support the experience that the Whyvillians have at Whyville and engage them. It may be that down the road they are interested in buying a car and they will think about Scion."

Because the Scion appeals to an unconventional consumer, Ms. Senior said, "a lot of what we do is based on the mind-set rather than the specific age group."

The power of younger consumers has grown stronger in recent years. According to research from Packaged Facts, a division of MarketResearch.com in Rockville, Md., 39 percent of parents of 10- and 11-year-olds say their children have a significant impact on brand purchases. Both boys and girls age 9 to 11 say they spend without thinking, and 9-to-11-year-olds account for 53 percent of total buying power among children 3 to 11. (They hope to keep spending, too—66 percent of boys age 9 to 11 say they want to be rich.)

Visitors to game sites like Whyville are generally open to product placement on the Web, many marketers say. According to a survey by comScore Media Metrix, only 15 percent of avid gamers said they would be unlikely to play games with product placements included.

But the key to reaching younger consumers, said Mr. Diamond of Alloy, is to capture them before they have any opinions on brands.

"Talk to the young person in their environment in a relevant way," he said. "I think too often advertisers wait to convert them later, and then it's too late."

5

Advertising Alone Cannot Be Blamed for Childhood Obesity

Chris Moerdyk

Chris Moerdyk is a marketing and media consultant. He is a regular contributor to AdVantage *online and the marketing columnist for the* Sunday Times *in South Africa.*

Advertising is not as harmful to youth as people often make it out to be. In fact, people should stop blaming advertising for causing childhood obesity and underage drinking and smoking, and start looking more closely at today's parents who do little to guide their children's life choices. Peer pressure also influences youths' consumer and behavioral choices more than advertising. Ads simply promote one brand name over another. They do not persuade people to do things they are not already doing.

If laws announced by the [South African] Health Department [in July 2007] are promulgated by parliament, it will become illegal to target children with advertising for junk or non-nutritional food.

Which will not only affect fast food outlets such as McDonald's and Wimpy but also a whole range of snacks and other foodstuffs with high sugar and fat content.

All of which will make advertising look even more like the villain it is already perceived to be, particularly by parents with young kids.

But really, is advertising as powerful as it is cracked up to be and is it such an evil influence? Or is there something else

Chris Moerdyk, "Adverts No Parental Substitute," *www.news24.com*, July 31, 2007. Reproduced by permission. www.news24.com.

that is making our kids fat, unhealthy and prone to such bad habits as smoking, drinking and drugs?

Parents Need to Take Some Blame

Frankly, while there is no doubt that there are some unscrupulous advertisers around today, they are few and far between.

And from what I can see, the reason we have so many fat, unhealthy kids who get involved in drugs and all sorts of other bad habits has got little to do with advertising and a lot to do with parents who don't give a darn what programmes their kids watch on TV or what movies they go to.

And who send them off to shopping malls or to school with lunch money without really caring about whether they have a proper lunch or just buy junk food. Nor do they care who their friends are.

These are also the parents who are so busy working either out of necessity or greed that they don't have time to guide and monitor their kids, and co-incidentally the greedy ones are also the parents who tend to yell loudest about wanting to ban advertising.

In short what they are wanting to do is get government to take responsibility for protecting their kids because they can't be bothered.

Peer Pressure Still Influences Kids

It is also a well known fact that when it comes to smoking, drinking, drugging, fashion, cell phones, music and all those other things that appeal to kids, whether they are two years old or twenty, advertising plays a relatively minor role compared with peer pressure.

Just ask your kids next time they pester you for something. I'll bet they won't say, "Oh I saw an ad for it" but rather "because my friend has got one".

Interestingly, in spite of drugs being such an enormous problem among our youth, I haven't ever seen a single ad for cocaine, dagga [marijuana]or tik [methamphetamine].

So, while advertising might not be entirely innocent of leading our youngsters astray, banning it won't really make much difference, if any, at all.

The real culprits are parents who don't have the time or the inclination to put a foot down when their kids tell them, "But Johnny's allowed to go to the mall. Johnny's allowed to see *that* movie."

It's all about being accepted and being cool. Kids don't just get into bad habits on their own—they're influenced almost entirely by their friends. Frankly, banning advertising is hardly worth bothering about.

But, it does allow politicians to score brownie points and give the impression that they're doing something positive.

Secondly, if advertising was so great an influence on kids, particularly teenagers and young adults, just where are they supposed to be seeing all this advertising?

It has been well documented that advertising is not a persuader but simply a promoter.

Advertising Simply Promotes Brands

Research data over the past decade has shown that the mass media has lost contact with the 16–24 year old market and that the number of youngsters in this category who read newspapers, listen to the radio or watch television is falling.

Quite difficult to be influenced by advertising when you don't see it.

It has been well documented that advertising is not a persuader but simply a promoter. For example, Colgate-Palmolive, one of the world's biggest advertisers, announced . . . that its profit rose 47% in the second quarter of [2007] and said that the reason was that effective cost-cutting measures had meant that they were able to spend a lot more on advertising.

But, that did not mean that all that extra advertising persuaded people to start using things like toothpaste and soap powder but just meant that a lot of people started using Colgate's products instead of those from competitors.

So, advertising certainly works. It must [work] because companies such as Pick 'n Pay, Coca-Cola, Toyota, Sony and other well known brands do not spend hundreds of millions of Rands [South African currency] on advertising just because they get a kick out of seeing their names up in lights.

In fact, they "invest" in advertising and can accurately predict what return they will have on their advertising investment.

But, that advertising does not persuade people to start drinking cold drinks, to drive cars, to start watching TV or to start consuming groceries. What it does is get people who already drink cold drinks, watch TV, buy groceries and drive cars to try Coke, Toyota, Sony and Pick 'n Pay.

Advertising is about choices—nothing else.

6

Humorous Advertisements Get Teens to Stop Smoking

Lianne George

Lianne George reports on culture and entertainment for Macleans, a national weekly current affairs magazine in Canada.

Antismoking ads with a sense of humor do a better job of preventing teenagers from smoking than the traditional, more somber ads from antismoking lobbyists in the past. Teens appreciate the dark humor of the American Legacy Foundation's award-winning "Truth" campaign that began airing in 1998. The campaign, which mocks tobacco industry executives, has been credited with reducing the incidence of teen smoking. As a result, other governments have adopted more edgy, less preachy approaches to their own antismoking campaigns.

Anti-smoking lobbyists have suddenly developed a sense of humour in their fight to get kids to butt out.

In July 2005, in an attempt to shock British youth into butting out en masse, the U.K. government unveiled a slick advertising campaign designed to subvert the deeply entrenched sex appeal of smoking. One of the ads, highlighting the link between smoking and male impotence, features a cigarette positioned suggestively between two "fingerlegs" with the tagline: "Your penis thinks you should stop smoking." Others in the series warn young women that not only will "fags" [cigarettes] give you yellow, "minging" [ugly] teeth, but

Lianne George, "Light(en)ing Up," *Maclean's*, vol. 118, August 22, 2005, p. 5C, 38–39. © 2005 by *Maclean's Magazine*. Reproduced by permission. www.socialsmokers.org/lightening_up.html.

that over time, the lip-puckering required for smoking will produce an undesirable wrinkling effect, colourfully described as "cat's bum mouth."

Suddenly, and improbably, the anti-smoking lobby has developed a sense of humour. In North America and abroad, the movement is producing some of the most irreverent, and even borderline raunchy, advertising to ever target youth—in print, online and on TV. Last November [2004], Ontario unveiled its "Stupid.ca" campaign, in which the act of smoking was equated with smearing oneself with dog feces. In Nova Scotia, the government launched a series of TV ads—part of its "Great Reasons to Smoke" campaign (www.sickofsmoke.com)—in which Terry and Dean, the hockey-haired hosers from the 2002 burnout movie FUBAR (F---ed Up Beyond All Recognition), wax idiotic about the social and economic benefits of tobacco usage (for instance, all of the smoke breaks land you an extra three days off a year if you add them up).

Youth are an entirely separate market and need to be addressed 'in their own language.'

Governments and non-profits, it seems, have finally grasped something consumer advertisers have known for years—that youth are an entirely separate market and need to be addressed "in their own language." They've also figured out that, for the *American Pie* generation, the worst fate imaginable is not pestilence or death, but looking like a schmuck in front of your friends. Coincidentally or not, the ads have dovetailed with dramatic declines in youth smoking rates.

Sombre Ads Make Smoking More Attractive

Historically, there were two approaches to urging young people not to smoke. First were the sombre you-smoke-you-die ads—featuring foreboding music and some part of the anatomy blackened and covered with lesions—which, aside from a momentary gross-out thrill, rolled right off the backs of kids in the prime of immortality. Then there were the hyper-earnest ads in which health ministries recruited squeaky-clean pop singers (such as Candi and Luba in Health Canada's "Break Free" campaign, circa 1985) to wag their fingers to dorky backbeats and dance on sound stages poorly disguised as gritty urban streets. Both approaches communicated the same message: adults think cigarettes are very, very bad. Which, for adolescents looking for easy ways to shock and disappoint their parents, just made smoking seem all the more attractive.

From an advertiser's perspective, anti-smoking messaging poses a particularly difficult challenge: to take something that's been perceived as cool since well before James Dean made it a symbol of disaffected youth everywhere, and make it uncool, even gauche. The American Legacy Foundation, a Washington-based non-profit group, pioneered the new anti-tobacco advertising with its award-winning "Truth" campaign, launched in 1998.

Developed by Arnold Worldwide, a top-tier U.S. agency whose clients include Hasbro and Volkswagen, the "Truth" campaign uses dark humour to take aim at the tobacco industry itself. The underlying message: "They're lying to you. What kind of an idiot do they take you for?" In a fake online sit-com, Fair Enough! (www.fairenough.com), actors parody smarmy tobacco executives in 60-second episodes, which are scripted with lines taken from the minutes of actual industry meetings and set to a tinny laugh track. During [2004]'s Super Bowl, one ad mocked the industry's belated concession that cigarette smoking is harmful to your health by featuring a fake company that manufactures frozen treats laced with shards of glass. "At Shards O'Glass Freezer Pops," says the mock executive, "our goal is to be the most responsible, effective and respected developer of glass shard consumer products intended for adults."

Evidence suggests "Truth" is achieving its goal. In 2002, the U.S. National Youth Tobacco Survey showed declines in high school smoking of 18 per cent over the previous two years. Research in the *American Journal of Public Health* found that there were approximately 300,000 fewer youth smokers in the U.S. by 2002, as a direct result of the campaign.

Teens Respond to Ads Featuring Peers

Inspired by that success, the Ontario government, with the help of Toronto advertising agency Bensimon Byrne and youth marketing firm Youthography, did some research of its own and found that the one thing young smokers and non-smokers agree on is that smoking is stupid. The resulting "Stupid.ca" campaign—aimed at tweens and young teens before they start—was created, with the help of a youth advisory commit-tee, to sound like kids talking to kids, so it would look com-pletely at home wedged between two MuchMusic videos. In one ad, a youth holds a lightning rod in the middle of a field during a lightning storm. In another, a teenage boy adorned with antlers tiptoes through the forest at the height of deer hunting season. There are no Ontario trillium logos or brought-to-you-bys to identify them as government fare.

'Kids don't want to hear health care messages from au-thority figures, but they will listen to messages about so-cial consequences from their peers.'

"We deliberately chose to focus on social factors," says health ministry spokesperson Kevin Finnerty, who admits the campaign, which includes TV, print and online components, was a little "edgy" for the government. "Our research told us that kids don't want to hear health care messages from au-thority figures, but they will listen to messages about social consequences from their peers." (Smokers' rights groups were outraged. Nancy Daigneault, president of Mychoice.ca, criticized the government for conceiving a "demeaning and disparaging" campaign. "I hope we do not see a repeat of the incredibly offensive and repugnant ad in which smokers are portrayed as smelling like—to use the exact quote—'dog crap.'")

Still, as in the U.S., attitudes of Canadian youth toward tobacco use appear to be changing. According to Health Canada, smoking among teens has decreased dramatically among 15- to 19-year-olds, from 28 per cent in 1999 to 18 per cent in 2004. This may be the cumulative result of a larger, multi-pronged attack, including stricter legislation, label warnings, and increased taxes. So while the originators of "Stupid.ca" can't claim sole credit for the decline, they know their audience is paying attention: they've had more than 600,000 unique visitors to the website since its launch in November.

"The idea is to create this new sort of brand identity around smoking," says Mike Farrell, director of research and strategy for Youthography, "as though it's just not something that anybody really does anymore—and you're kind of old-school or old-fashioned by doing it."

Ironically, just as Canada is cracking down on tobacco use, it's showing less of an interest in marijuana consumption— and as a result, say some experts, young people are perceiving the latter as a significantly less dangerous habit. "Pot smoking," says Farrell, "has gone up massively among youth."

7

Innovative Advertisements Can Prevent Teen Smoking

Theresa Howard

Theresa Howard covers advertising for USA Today *for which she writes the weekly Ad Track column. She also has worked as a senior editor covering marketing news for* Brandweek *magazine.*

The American Legacy Foundation's "Truth" campaign strives to make being anti-smoking a cool thing among teens. Rather than hitting the airwaves with stark statistics, the ads personalize the negative impact of smoking through concrete images teens can relate to. Although some studies suggest that the campaign's impact is starting to wane, it is credited with decreasing teen smoking nationwide.

Marketers spend billions each year in a highly competitive marketplace to convince teens they need or want such products as cell phones, trendy apparel, tech gadgets, snacks and soft drinks.

That's an easy job compared with selling teens on the idea that there are products that they *don't* want to go near.

The goal of the American Legacy Foundation, which uses selling tactics similar to those used by consumer marketers, is to sell teens on not smoking cigarettes.

The group's "Truth" ad campaign tries to show teens the dark side of smoking by exposing the marketing tactics of tobacco companies. The high-profile campaign included buying ads on the Super Bowl in 2004.

The methodology: TV advertising created with the intent of having a credible message that taps into the "in" crowd and tries to make it cool to be anti-smoking.

Leveraging peer pressure is an important way to reach a demographic in which "hanging out with friends" ranks among the top activities of both boys and girls, according to a teen survey in 2003 by research group BuzzBack. And 68% of teens classify themselves in one of three groups: socialites, outsiders or academics.

The foundation, with help from ad agencies Crispin Porter + Bogusky, Miami, and Arnold Worldwide, Boston, developed grainy, documentary-style ads that inform teens about the health aspects of smoking, without preaching. "You don't have to be much of a social scientist to recognize that saying, 'I dare you to do something,' is almost a guarantee that young people will rebel," says Chris Cullen, executive vice president, marketing and communications.

Getting Into the "In" Crowd

By recognizing that "the No. 1 thing on their minds is the crowd they are in, what's my circle and how hard do I have to work to be in it," Cullen says, the Truth campaign has gotten "into the in crowd. We are privileged to have an inside conversation with 12- to 17-year-olds."

The foundation can afford that privilege thanks to $1.8 billion from the $200 billion settlement reached in 1998 between 46 state attorneys general and tobacco companies.

American Legacy spends about $100 million annually on anti-smoking messages in TV ads, grass-roots events and on the Web.

"The Web's a huge part of Truth," says Alex Bogusky, creative director and partner at Crispin Porter + Bogusky. "You don't have to do the job in one 30-second ad because you've done pieces of it all over the landscape over the last two years."

Two recent TV ads show teens lining up mannequins on a busy street to represent "replacement smokers"—new smokers who cigarette companies try to get to replace smokers who die. The ad closes on a girl whose father died from smoking-related illnesses. She points out that she hasn't found a replacement for her dad.

In another ad, teens survey people on the street and take their photo if they say they know anyone affected by smoking. The ad closes with Lucy Abbott, who introduces herself as someone waiting for a lung transplant and says: "If you didn't know someone before, you do now."

Earlier ads in the campaign looked at the numbers of Americans affected by smoking-related illnesses. The latest ads aim to personalize the impact.

[Teens] told us to show them a way to think about 1,200 [smoking-related] daily deaths.

"At some point (teens) seem distanced by the facts," Cullen says. "They told us to show them a way to think about 1,200 daily deaths."

The TV ads were very popular with consumers surveyed by Ad Track, *USA TODAY*'s weekly poll—particularly 18- to 24-year-olds, the youngest age group in the survey.

Of those familiar with the ads, 39% overall like the ads "a lot." And for those ages 18 to 24, 43% like the ads a lot—more than double the Ad Track average of 21%. Though Legacy's core target is 12- to 17-year-olds, Cullen is glad the ads resonate widely, but says the ad-buying strategy focuses on teens.

"We are going to be talking to a broad audience of young people, but we make our media decisions based on the at-risk, rebellious, independence-seeking teens open to smoking," Cullen says.

The ads may have helped cut teen smoking in recent years, but the impact may be beginning to wane. After teen smoking fell by half since the mid-1990s, the 2003 University of Michigan Monitoring the Future Study released in December reported the "rate of declines is slowing appreciably."

But American Legacy will release a study . . . that has "clear evidence that the Truth campaign has accelerated the rate of decline in youth smoking," Chief Executive Cheryl Healton says.

Demonstrating results is key to American Legacy's hunt for new sources of funding. The non-profit's settlement funding is over in 2008, Healton says. "In another four years we won't be able to afford such a campaign (as Truth). If it stayed on the air, it would be at a much lower level."

8

Junk Food Advertising Is Contributing to Childhood Obesity

Elizabeth Olson

Elizabeth Olson is a staff writer for the New York Times. *She frequently covers foreign affairs, business, and American culture.*

Advertisements for junk food have infiltrated television programming aimed at children and teens. These ads for candy, sugary snacks, and fast food are encouraging American children to maintain an unhealthy diet, contributing to the nation's childhood obesity problem. The food industry supports health groups' push toward marketing a healthier lifestyle to children and teens. These groups propose public service announcements that promote fitness and nutrition.

Can television ads aimed at children finally go on a healthy diet?

For years, health officials have warned that bombarding children with junk food commercials has contributed to the problem of childhood obesity. Food conglomerates, eager to fend off federal regulation, have made various commitments to improve, including a pledge in December [2007] to meet goals for promoting fitness and healthier foods.

The Kaiser Family Foundation released a study [in March 2007] that it said provides a way to measure the companies' progress. The foundation, a nonprofit group that focuses on health care issues, found that 50 percent of ad time on children's shows is devoted to food. Among the ads aimed at children and teenagers, 72 percent are for candy, snacks, sugary cereals or fast food.

These advertisements "are largely for products that children should be eating less of, not more of, if we're going to get a handle on childhood obesity," said Victoria J. Rideout, director of the foundation's program for the study of entertainment media and health.

The study's results were presented at a two-hour event in Washington that featured recorded ads for products like Kellog's Cocoa Krispies, Frito-Lay's Twisted Cheetos and Nestle's Crunch bars. According to Kaiser, only 4 percent of the ads it viewed were for dairy products and 1 percent for fruit juices. There were none for fruits or vegetables.

Food and advertising executives said that the data in the study, which looked at 2,613 ads on 13 television networks from May to September of 2005, was old and that the industry had made progress since then.

"This was a very good snapshot of 2005," said Nancy R. Green, PepsiCo's vice president for health and wellness policy and nutrition technology, who spoke on a panel discussing the study's findings. "But less than 1 percent of our marketing goes to children. And we are moving to advertise our healthier products." PepsiCo owns brands like Tropicana and Quaker.

Daniel L. Jaffe, executive vice president of the Association of National Advertisers, said the study ignored changes companies have made to minimize the exposure of less nutritious products.

"There have been changes in the marketplace over the past 18 months that included the introduction of new and reformulated products," he said, referring, for example, to products that are lower in calories, sodium or sugar, or that contain whole grains.

The Kaiser study, which was conducted by Indiana University under Ms. Rideout's direction, found that food is, by far, the most ubiquitous product advertised to children, followed by media, which includes movies, video games and music. Of the food ads that the study examined, 34 percent were for candy and snacks, 28 percent for cereal and 10 percent for fast food. Ms. Rideout said that almost 100 percent of the cereals were sugared.

Kids View Thousands of Food Ads

Tweens, or children in the 8-to-12 age group, see more food ads than younger children or teenagers, the study found. Children age 8 to 12 view 21 television ads for food products every day, adding up to more than 7,600 ads a year.

Teenagers—13 to 18—view 17 [food ads] a day, or about 6,000 a year.

Children in the 2-to-7 age range see 12 food ads a day, or about 4,400 a year. Teenagers—13 to 18—view 17 such commercials a day, or about 6,000 a year.

The tween total was higher, Ms. Rideout said, because they watch not only children's channels but also other programming, including reality shows and situation comedies.

Growing awareness of childhood obesity has galvanized health-related groups to press big food marketers to cut back on junk food advertising to children. Groups that have voiced concern include the American Academy of Pediatrics, which called for a ban on ads for junk food aimed at young children, as well as the Federal Trade Commission, the Department of Health and Human Services, and the Institute of Medicine, a nonprofit group.

In December [2006] 11 large companies, including PepsiCo, Kraft Foods and McDonald's, agreed to adopt voluntary rules to make healthier foods or healthier lifestyles the subject of at least 50 percent of all advertising aimed at children 12 and under, said C. Lee Peeler, president of the National Advertising Review Council.

The rules did not give specific definitions of healthiness, but, under the arrangement, each company will set its own goals, he said. The Children's Food and Beverage Advertising Initiative, which Mr. Peeler also leads, aims to have companies make pledges by summer or early fall [of 2007] he said.

Ms. Rideout said that the Kaiser study would help measure whether those initiatives lead to any real changes in advertising content.

The Federal Communications Commission also has a task force to examine the impact of the media on childhood obesity; its members include the Walt Disney Company, General Mills and PepsiCo along with representatives of health and consumer groups.

Childhood Obesity Is a Problem

Senator Sam Brownback of Kansas, who helped form the task force, spoke at the Kaiser event yesterday [March 28, 2007,] and warned that obesity in children was such a grave problem that government regulations could be required if advertisers did not make noticeable changes.

"We need to see some objective numbers," said Mr. Brownback, a Republican presidential candidate. "We've just got to see these obesity numbers go down."

The food industry has proposed more public service announcements promoting fitness and nutrition.

The food industry has proposed more public service announcements promoting fitness and nutrition. But the Kaiser study found that children see few of these messages: one every few days for children under age 8, compared with 26 food ads in the same time period. For tweens, the ratio is one for every 48 food commercials, and for teenagers, one announcement for every 130 food ads.

Ms. Rideout said there was a role for public announcements, "but such educational campaigns should have limited expectations, or a substantial budget."

The study also examined the ways the ads tried to appeal to children and teenagers. The most common appeal, said Walter Gantz of Indiana University, the author of the study, was taste—"cinnamony," for example—a feature that was highlighted in 34 percent of the commercials. Fun came in second (18 percent), followed by premiums or contests (16 percent) then the newness or uniqueness of a product (10 percent). Only 2 percent of the ads mentioned health or nutrition as a primary or secondary appealing factor, and 5 percent mentioned gaining strength or energy; other categories measured included convenience and enjoyment.

The ads were recorded on the commercial networks, including ABC, NBC, CBS, and Fox; commercial cable, including MTV, BET, Nickelodeon and Cartoon Network; and PBS. They were chosen according to Nielsen Media Research data for the top 10 networks in each age group.

9

Television Advertising May Play a Role in Childhood Obesity

Sonia Livingstone

Sonia Livingstone is Professor of Social Psychology and a member of the Department of Media and Communications at the London School of Economics and Political Science.

Since 1989, obesity among youth in Britain and the United States has tripled. A number of factors can account for this dramatic increase in obesity rates, but studies suggest that television promotion of foods high in fat, sugar, and salt is partially to blame for children's unhealthy food preferences. Governments in Britain and America are considering following Sweden's example of banning advertisements of junk food to children. Although research finds only a modest but consistent link between television viewing and obesity among children and teenagers, the link is strong enough to warrant restrictions on food advertising to children.

There is growing public concern over rising levels of obesity among children, in the UK and many other countries in the developed world, as World Health Organization reports have warned. The Royal College of Physicians reports that obesity doubled among two to four year olds between 1989 and 1998, and trebled [tripled] among six to fifteen year olds between 1990 and 2002 in the UK. Similarly, in the US, obe-

Sonia Livingstone, "Does TV Advertising Make Children Fat?" *Public Policy Research*, vol. 13, March/May 2006, p. 54–60. Copyright © 2006 the author. Journal compilation copyright © 2006 IPPR. Reproduced by permission of Blackwell Publishers.

sity among six to nineteen year olds has trebled over the past four decades, to 16 per cent in 1999–2002, while the incidence of type 2 diabetes has doubled in the past decade, with notable increases also in the risk of heart disease, stroke, circulatory problems, some cancers, osteoporosis and blindness.

Researchers are generally agreed that multiple factors account for childhood obesity, including individual, social, environmental, and cultural factors.

The evidence of rising obesity, it seems, is beyond question. The explanation is less clear. The US's Institute of Medicine's (IOM) Committee on Food Marketing and the Diets of Children and Youth observed in its major report to Congress (2005) that children's diets 'result from the interplay of many factors . . . all of which, apart from genetic predispositions, have undergone significant transformations over the past three decades'. In other words, researchers are generally agreed that multiple factors account for childhood obesity, including individual, social, environmental and cultural factors. These factors are, for the most part, subject to change, and many of them interact with each other in complex ways not yet well understood.

One consequence is that policy decisions regarding intervention are highly contested, because multiple stakeholders, with competing interests, are involved. It is in this context that this essay focuses on just one putative explanation for childhood obesity, namely food promotion, particularly television advertising of foods high in fat, salt or sugar. It asks one key question: is the evidence base linking advertising to children's health sufficient to guide policy decisions?

Why Blame Television Advertising?

Everyone agrees that the food industry is a major player in the advertising market. The total UK advertising spending per annum [year] in the categories of food, soft drinks and chain restaurants is £743 million, with £522 million spent on television advertising and £32 million spent in children's airtime. In the US, figures are much greater: for food and beverage marketing, US $11 billion was spent on advertising in 2004, including US $5 billion on television advertising, in addition to the larger but rarely calculated amounts spent on other marketing investments (product placement, character licensing, in-school activities, 'advergames' and so on).

Most advertising to children is for products high in fat, salt and sugar, [therefore] this influence is . . . harmful to children's health.

Consequently, considerable research efforts have been devoted to the hypothesised causal relationship between food promotion and children's food preferences, diet and health. Systematic and substantial reviews of the best empirical studies argue that television advertising, the subject of most research, contributes to the unhealthy food preferences, poor diet and, consequently, growing obesity among children in Western societies. Thus, in the UK, G. Hastings *et al*'s [2003] recent systematic review for the Food Standards Agency concluded that 'food promotion is having an effect, particularly on children's preferences, purchase behaviour and consumption. This effect is independent of other factors and operates at both a brand and category level'. Noting that most advertising to children is for products high in fat, salt and sugar, this influence is, they conclude further, harmful to children's health. The US's Institute of Medicine (2005) report concluded, more strongly still, that 'among many other factors, food and beverage marketing influences the preferences and purchase requests of children, influences consumption at least in the short term, is a likely contributor to less healthful diets, and may contribute to negative diet-related health outcomes and risks among children and youth'.

Not everyone agrees with these conclusions, and there are some significant dissenting voices, on various grounds, from industry, public policy makers and the academy. Nonetheless, as the evidence for the harmful effects of food advertising on children's health accumulates across Europe, North America and elsewhere, there is a growing consensus that the evidence base is sufficient to guide policy, and that it is time some tough policy decisions were taken.

From Evidence to Policy

For many, the link from evidence to policy is clear. As the World Health Organization (2003) urges: 'Food and beverage advertisements should not exploit children's inexperience or credulity. Messages that encourage unhealthy dietary practices or physical inactivity should be discouraged, and positive healthy messages encouraged'. The British Medical Association, responding to the Government's White Paper, *Choosing Health: Making Healthier Choices Easier* (November 2004), has recommended an outright ban on advertising foods to children in the UK. This goes a crucial step beyond the White Paper, which suggested a voluntary period of modification of advertising foods to children, giving food advertisers until 2007 before reconsidering the question of a ban.

The Office of Communications (Ofcom) is currently consulting on the degree to which food advertising to children should be restricted, noting that this has direct costs for broadcasters in terms of revenues available for children's programming. In the US, the Institute of Medicine report to Congress recommended that, 'if voluntary efforts related to advertising during children's television programming are unsuccessful in shifting the emphasis away from high-calorie and low-nutrient foods and beverages to the advertising of healthful foods and beverages, Congress should engage legislation mandating the shift on both broadcast and cable television'. In some countries (Sweden, most notably), such a ban is already in force.

A ban on advertising foods high in fat, sugar and salt to children is not the only policy under consideration, particularly as the evidence is far from clear that bans are effective in altering children's diets (this is partly because few countries have implemented a truly effective ban on food advertising and this has impeded evaluation research). The Institute of Medicine recommends numerous parallel strategies, including calling for marketing resources to promote healthy diets, improving food labelling systems, and developing explicit industry self-regulatory guidelines for new forms of marketing communications. Research and policy advisers in the UK and elsewhere have also proposed media literacy programmes to enhance children's critical analysis of marketing, targeting parents to encourage them to modify their own, and their children's, diets, encouraging alternatives to prolonged exposure to television on the part of both parents and children, making healthier foods cheaper, promoting exercise and healthy lifestyles, and so on.

The Limits of Evidence

Undoubtedly, these are all sensible policy proposals. Yet it should be acknowledged that the evidence for their likely effectiveness is variable, and requires further research. Most research has been basic rather than applied, devoted to establishing the claimed causal link between advertising and food choice, rather than to evaluating the effectiveness of specific intervention. Media literacy programmes, for example, have not been clearly shown to alter behavioural choices, and the evidence that reducing exposure to advertising has beneficial consequences is also mixed.

Worryingly, the temptation to seek simple solutions—such as scapegoating television or computer games as the major culprits, instead of acknowledging that multiple factors are at work—distracts attention from the breadth of strategies required for sustained and targeted interventions, as well as from the diversity of research required to guide their implementation. So, we do not, at present, have a clear consensus regarding the range of influences on children's food choice, though these are often taken to include gender, food costs, birth order, cultural meanings of food, obesity levels, family eating habits, parental regulation of media, parental mediation of advertising, peer norms, pro-health messages and pester power. Nor, more importantly, is there evidence that weighs these factors against each other so as to determine their relative influence.

It is, therefore, problematic to claim too much for the evidence base, for it renders those in favour of intervention vulnerable to the always-ready charge of overstating their case, common enough charge in the often fraught field of media effects.

In my reviews of the literature for Ofcom, I argued that the balance of evidence does support the conclusion that television advertising has a modest direct effect on children's food choices. I concluded that there is insufficient evidence to show that television advertising, indeed food promotion more generally, has the larger, indirect effects (through the interaction between promotion and other factors affecting children's lives) that many in the fields of child psychology and consumer research believe occur.

There will never be the ideal experiment to resolve all doubt . . . that television advertising adversely affects children's food choice.

The conclusion in favour of modest direct effects rests on two premises. First, that there will never be the ideal experiment to resolve all doubt and so determine, once and for all, that television advertising adversely affects children's food choice. Second, that policy must therefore err on the side of caution, based on a balance of probabilities as specified by the precautionary principle. In short, this domain is no different from many others in which policy rests on a judgement of probable influence rather than awaiting a scientific 'answer' regarding the harmful effects of food promotion, as the Chief Medical Officer has pointed out. In proceeding on this basis, it is important to understand clearly just what the empirical research does and does not show.

The Evidence

The growing concern regarding the link between marketing/ advertising and adverse health consequences is resulting in a growing number of population surveys concerned with obesity that include a measure of television viewing. A 34-nation study of ten to sixteen year olds in 2001–02 found that, in 22 of the 34 countries (including the UK, where obesity figures are relatively high), there is a significant positive relationship between Body Mass Index (BMI) and amount of viewing. Indeed, many large-scale, well-conducted national surveys, mainly but not only in the US, also find a modest but consistent association between hours spent watching television and the likelihood of being overweight among children and teenagers.

The amount of weekend television viewing in early childhood continues to influence BMI [Body Mass Index] in adulthood.

Although experimental designs permit stronger causal claims to be made about the effects of advertising, the research effort has shifted from experimental to national survey methods, taking the causal hypothesis to have been established and so turning to investigate the range of factors, including but not restricted to advertising, that together influence children's diet and health. Large scale studies are needed here because many of these factors—including television advertising—each exert a fairly small influence. Further, longitudinal research—of which there is a growing amount—tracks year-on-year changes, showing the cumulative effects of advertising over years or decades. For example, a cohort study of over 10,000 nine to fourteen year olds in the US found that those who spent more time with television/videos/games showed larger BMI increases a year later. These effects were stronger for those who are already overweight, suggesting a cumulative effect over time. The British Birth Cohort study, similarly, followed up over 11,000 children from the ages of five to 30, revealing that the amount of weekend television viewing in early childhood continues to influence BMI in adulthood.

The survey evidence, showing small but consistent effects of exposure to television, is mirrored by the experimental evidence. This too suggests that television advertising has a modest, direct effect on children's food choices, such that those who are exposed to particular messages are influenced in their food preferences and choices (as exhibited in the experimental situation), compared with those who did not see those messages.

Some experimental research continues to be conducted. In the UK, J. Halford *et al* (2004) recently showed 42 children aged nine to eleven advertisements for either food or nonfood items. Afterwards, the children ate significantly more after exposure to the food advertisements, and the obese and overweight children in the sample were particularly likely to remember the food advertisements. In another UK experiment, S. Auty and C. Lewis (2004) showed 105 children (aged six to seven and eleven to twelve) a scene from the film, *Home Alone*, in which Pepsi Cola was spilled, while a control group saw the same clip with no branded product. The experimental group were significantly more likely to select Pepsi rather than Coke afterwards, compared to the control group.

Earlier research, conducted mainly in the US, shows similar kinds of findings, albeit not consistently. Not all experiments are conducted in the artificial surroundings of a laboratory either. For example, in a much cited naturalistic experiment conducted over two weeks with five to eight year olds at a summer camp in Quebec, G. Gom and M. Goldberg (1982) found that showing adverts for fruit resulted in children drinking more orange juice, while adverts for sweets resulted in them drinking less orange juice. In another experiment, B. Greenberg and J. Brand (1993) compared the responses of fifteen to sixteen year olds in matched schools, one which received Channel One, one which did not. They found that viewers of Channel One evaluated products advertised on the channel more favourably than did non-viewers and that they named more of the advertised brands as products they intended to buy, although actual purchases did not differ between viewers and non-viewers.

Experiments can also be used to evaluate interventions, though this is less common. T. Robinson (1999) provided a range of school-based interventions to third and fourth grade children (approximately seven-to-eight-years-old) to reduce their television viewing and videogame playing over a six-month period. Compared with the control group, the experimental group not only reduced their television viewing but also showed reduced BMI and adiposity (measure of body fat). Curiously, there was no reduction in high-fat foods, snacking or highly advertised foods in the diet of the experimental group.

What the Evidence Can Show

The differences between surveys and experiments are important. Although this is not the place for a detailed account of epistemological or methodological issues in empirical research, some points are worth noting. . . .

First, experiments tend to link advertising to the precursors of diet and health, namely food-related beliefs and preferences, rather than to behaviour directly. The link from food preferences to health remains an inference, therefore, though not an unreasonable one. Further, few experiments have been conducted on teenagers, leaving most causal claims focused on the effects of advertising on children. Although more public concern is concentrated on children, obesity affects all ages, and there is little reason to suppose that teenagers (and, indeed, adults) are unaffected by advertising. Indeed, as I have argued elsewhere, it seems likely that different age groups are differently but still successfully targeted by advertising, with promotional strategies tailored to specific interests and age groups.

The limitation of surveys, although often rigorously conducted on a substantial scale, is also evident from the table. Among the many influences on obesity, television viewing is consistently reported as making an independent contribution (that is, controlling for other factors) to children's and teenagers' weight/obesity in range of countries. However, the measure used for television exposure—generally a simple estimate of hours per week—is a poor proxy for exposure to advertising in particular. Thus survey evidence does not distinguish among three possible explanations for the observed association between television exposure and diet/health/obesity: (1) television viewing results in exposure to advertisements for food high in fat, salt or sugar; (2) television viewing is associated with frequent snacking, pre-prepared meals and/or fast food consumption; and (3) television viewing is a sedentary activity that reduces metabolic rates and displaces physical exercise. There is some support for each of these explanations, although little empirical research attempts to disentangle them, and many researchers believe all three to be operating.

Last, for those concerned with the validity and generalisability of research studies ... most studies have faced a clear trade-off between using a research design that supports causal inferences (with random allocation of participants to experiment or control groups, in which media exposure is followed by measurement of the outcome variable) and a research design that is 'ecologically valid' (conducted under conditions that resemble everyday life and so permit generalisation to the population). Put simply, with purely correlational evidence, the direction of causality and the problem of third causes, is difficult to resolve. With purely experimental evidence, the claim that findings can be generalised to the everyday lives of children is difficult to sustain. On the other hand, to put the same point positively, with a correlational study, one can demonstrate the existence of an association between exposure and behaviour under naturalistic conditions. With an experiment one can demonstrate the existence of a causal effect of exposure on behaviour under controlled conditions. Hence researchers tend to use both types of design, 'triangulating' the findings from each in drawing overall conclusions.

Policy Implications

So, where does this leave policy? Although policy decisions must here, as always, be made in the absence of the 'perfect' test, use of the precautionary principle does support the restriction of food advertising to children. Research provides little guidance regarding the influence of forms of promotion other than television advertising (whether using old or new media platforms), for this has rarely been examined, notwithstanding the fast-changing array of promotional strategies, particularly for the internet, games, mobile phone and so on. Nor does research on television advertising offer straightforward guidance regarding the degree of restriction, partly because there is no easy translation from amount of advertising viewed to dietary consequences, and partly because little research has evaluated the relative importance of food advertising by comparison with other influences on diet. However, there are some indications to guide regulators and other stakeholders in determining how much emphasis to place on food advertising, as part of a multi-stranded policy framework.

For every additional hour of daily television viewing . . . the prevalence of teenage obesity could increase by 2 percent.

Generally, the measured size of the effect (a statistical term referring to a standardised index of magnitude) in empirical research is small to medium. This is the case for both experiments (generally, on television advertising) and for surveys (generally, on overall television exposure). However, many researchers are concerned to stress that 'small' effects in statistical terms add up to a large number of children in absolute terms, with the cumulative effects over the period of a child's development being much more sizeable, as some longitudinal research is beginning to show. For example, M. Storey *et al* (2002) estimated that, for every additional hour of daily television viewing, BMI could increase by 0.2. Put another way, for every additional hour of daily television viewing, W. Dietz and S. Gortmaker (1985) estimated the prevalence of teenage obesity could increase by 2 per cent. This is not such a small figure considering that, in the US, this would mean an estimated additional 1.5 million young people falling into the 'obese' category.

Given the complex array of factors contributing to the rise in childhood obesity, a different approach is recommended. If research and policy continues to ask simply, 'does food promotion affect children's food preferences, knowledge and behaviour?', I suggest that the debate will continue to be polarised, with calls for new and better research followed by continued but irresolvable methodological disputes. In other words, very little policy will actually happen.

Alternatively, one can ask, what factors affect children's food preferences, knowledge and behaviour? This requires a refocusing on a probabilistic assessment of the range of risks to children's health and should take us into a broader and potentially more productive discussion of the different factors involved in children's food choice, as part of a risk-based approach to assessing potential media harms. In relation to the question of whether television advertising contributes to the problem of childhood obesity, a risk-based approach would recognise, and weigh, the role of television advertising, placing it in a multifactor context. And, as I have argued, this approach would support taking policy action on television advertising aimed specifically at children as one among a number of important ways forward.

10

Teens and Parents Should Be Wary of Military Marketing

Josh Golin

Writer Josh Golin is an anticommercialism and antiwar activist from Arlington, Massachusetts. He is the program manager at the Campaign for a Commercial-Free Childhood at the Judge Baker Children's Center in Boston.

In an effort to boost its enlistment numbers, the United States Army has adopted corporate advertising tactics to market itself to teens. It is striving to increase its brand recognition among American youth through the use of video games, peer influencers, and advertisements on Channel One, an educational television station viewed in children's classrooms nationwide. The decision to join the army is a life-altering one that should not be taken as lightly as choosing between brands of soda. Teens should be more aware of the army's recruiting tactics and seek out more information before making the decision to enlist.

As the war in Iraq stretches into its 31st month [in the fall of 2005] the United States military is facing serious recruiting shortages. The branches of the military that supply the largest number of troops to Iraq have had the most difficulties with recruiting. The Army failed to reach its recruiting goals in four out of the first six months of 2005; the Army National Guard came up short in all six.

To keep up with the demand for troops, the military has increased its marketing in an attempt to sell youth on the idea of enlisting. The Army, for instance, has nearly doubled its advertising budget since 2000. Recruitment advertising has also become more sophisticated as military marketers increasingly use techniques perfected by the $15 billion-a-year youth marketing industry. Colonel Thomas Nickerson, the Army's advertising director, recently told the *New York Times*, that the Army's marketing campaigns use "the best practices of corporate America."

Some might question, however, whether emulating these "best practices" is in the best interests of children and their families. After all, the alarming epidemic of childhood obesity, youth violence, precocious and irresponsible sexuality, excessive materialism, and family stress have all been linked to youth-directed marketing. Just as youth marketers use new media, in-school advertising, and viral marketing in order to make an end-run around parents to target children with junk food, violent media and other potentially harmful products, the military is increasingly using these same techniques to sell youth on potentially harmful military service.

In-school Marketing

Youth marketers like targeting children in schools because they have a captive audience that is unable to avoid their commercial messages. One of the more popular—and controversial—ways that students are exposed to advertising in schools is through Channel One. According to its website, Channel One's newscasts—which consist of ten minutes of news and two minutes of commercials—are shown in nearly 12,000 schools to almost eight million students each school day.

The military is one of the leading advertisers on Channel One; one study found that ten percent of the broadcast's ads were for military recruitment. This year [2005], the Army alone will spend more than $2 million dollars on advertising and promotions with Channel One, and the Marines and

Navy are regular advertisers as well. The Army also sponsors content on Channel One during Black History and Hispanic Heritage Months that highlight the contributions of African-American and Hispanic soldiers throughout history. Such an arrangement follows a trend favored by corporate marketers where the lines between content and advertising are increasingly blurred. It also allows the Army to target their message to two minority groups that make up a disproportionate percentage of the troops in Iraq.

The military—like corporations—is interested in cradle-to-grave branding.

The military is also following the corporate model by targeting their commercial messages to younger and younger children. For instance, despite the fact the Army claims they only advertise to children 16 and older, their ads on Channel One are shown to children in grades 7–12. The Army also advertises in in-school publications, such as Scholastic's *Science World*, which are distributed to children as young as sixth graders. And in the latest indication that the military—like corporations—is interested in cradle-to-grave branding, a promotional film made by the Department of Defense has been showing regularly at Chuck E. Cheese, a party center for young children.

Using New Technologies

New technologies have allowed marketers to move beyond television to target youth through a variety of means. Food marketers, for instance, are particularly fond of "advergames," computer games built completely around products that keep children's attention focused on specific brands much longer than traditional commercials. Similarly, the Army's recruiting website also includes a section for visitors to play and download Army branded games.

The most popular of these games is America's Army, a first-person shooter game that allows players to simulate the life of a soldier from basic training to combat. Since its release a little more than three years ago, America's Army has been downloaded more than 16 million times. The Army has referred to the game as its best recruiting tool and now organizes regular recruiting events featuring America's Army tournaments for players ages 13 and up.

It is not surprising that the Army would want to cash in on the tremendous popularity of violent video games among youth. There is something particularly disturbing, however, about using a game where all deaths are virtual in order to promote a career choice where the possibility of real killing, death and serious injuries exist. Last year [2004], the national advocacy group Veterans for Peace adopted a resolution condemning the Army's use of video games for recruitment purposes.

Viral Marketing

In recent years, corporations have begun tapping into existing youth social hierarchies in order to market their products more effectively. Marketers seek out popular kids and give them free products to market to their (often unsuspecting) friends, a technique known as viral marketing. Similarly, the Nation reports that the US Army's recruiting handbook urges recruiters to "Know your student influencers. . . . some influential students such as the student president or the captain of the football team may not enlist: however, they can and will provide you with referrals that will enlist." Recruiters are also encouraged to integrate themselves seamlessly into students' lives. Suggestions include volunteering to help coach athletic teams, chaperone dances, and to "get involved with Boy Scout troops."

Undermining Parents

One of the reasons corporations like to market to children is that so many of their products—junk food, violent media, sexualized clothing—are likely to meet with parental disapproval. Military marketing also undermines parents' authority as gatekeepers by targeting youth directly, even those parents who have taken active measures to insure that recruiters do not contact their children.

Parents cannot opt their children out of the mandatory viewing of military ads on Channel One or prevent them from being solicited by a recruiter masquerading as a football coach.

A provision in the No Child Left Behind Act gives parents (and students over the age of 18) the ability to "opt-out" of military recruiting. Parents can write to their school district and ask that their child's personal information not be turned over to military recruiters. But parents cannot opt their children out of the mandatory viewing of military ads on Channel One or prevent them from being solicited by a recruiter masquerading as a football coach.

The military also has other ways of acquiring students' personal information. The Pentagon has hired BeNow, a private marketing firm, to maintain a database of 30 million young people ages 16–25—including those students who have opted out of military recruitment through the No Child Left Behind provision. The database includes names, addresses, email addresses, ethnicity, social security numbers, areas of study and cell phone numbers. Many advertisers view cell phones as the next great marketing medium so don't be surprised if the military starts sending games and text messages to teens and children directly through their phones.

What's Wrong with Military Branding?

Responding to critics who charged that the America's Army videogame was a sinister way of targeting young children, a veteran recruiter told the *Seattle Times*, "This isn't some kind of psychological thing to brainwash anybody. It's getting the U.S. Army name out there in a positive light. It's like Coca-Cola. You see the shape of the bottle and you know what it is. It's branding."

It isn't only brainwashing, however, that is cause for concern; branding is bad enough. Marketers promote brand identification to get consumers to differentiate between remarkably similar products (e.g. Coke and Pepsi) and to make purchases based on emotions and positive associations rather than careful consideration of the benefits, costs, and potentially harmful effects of a product. In other words, branding discourages critical thinking, the very skill that young people will need before making what may be the most important decision of their young lives.

Potential military recruits should seek out as much information from as many sources as possible.

Potential military recruits should seek out as much information from as many sources as possible. Before enlisting, they should understand why the military is having such a tough time finding new recruits. They should be aware that they will most likely be sent to Iraq if they enlist. They should understand that the war is not going well, and that there is no end in sight to a conflict in which [as of late 2005] nearly 2,000 Americans have died and thousands more have been injured. They should recognize that they will be trained to kill; and that the very real possibility exists that they themselves will be seriously injured or killed. None of this crucial information is likely to be found in a video game promoting the Army brand or on Channel One.

Younger children who are not yet capable of making such difficult and complex decisions should simply be left alone by military recruiters and marketers. Older children should be actively assisted by their parents in their decision-making process. And both parents and children should be wary of anyone who acts as if the decision to enlist is like choosing between two brands of soda.

Organizations to Contact

The editors have compiled the following list of organizations concerned with the issues debated in this book. The descriptions are derived from materials provided by the organizations. All have publications or information available for interested readers. The list was compiled on the date of publications of the present volume; the information provided here may change. Be aware that many organizations may take several weeks or longer to respond to inquiries, so allow as much time as possible.

About-Face
PO Box 77665, San Francisco, CA   94107
(415) 436-0212
e-mail: info@about-face.org
Web site: www.about-face.org

About-Face is an organization dedicated to combating negative effects associated with the media's stereotypical portrayal of women. Through education and outreach, About-Face encourages women and girls to become more media literate and reject the unattainable ideals and objectification of women in advertisements. The organization's Web site provides galleries of positive and negative ads, as well as fact sheets on topics such as body image, children and the media, and appearance messages.

Adbusters Media Foundation
1243 W. Seventh Ave., Vancouver, BC   V6H 1B7
   Canada
(604) 736-9401 • fax: (604) 737-6021
e-mail: info@adbusters.org
Web site: www.adbusters.org

Adbusters Media Foundation is a network of concerned individuals worldwide who promote large-scale social change through educational projects that are meant to infuriate individuals and in turn serve as a catalyst for social activism. One overriding concern of the foundation is the intense commercialization and consumerism associated with large corporations and the media. To this end, the network has organized the Buy Nothing Day and TV Turnoff Week campaigns to provide individuals with the opportunity to take action. The foundation publishes the magazine *Adbusters.*

Ad Council

261 Madison Ave., 11th Fl., New York, NY 10016
(212) 922-1500
Web site: www.adcouncil.org

The Ad Council has been producing public service announcements (PSAs) since 1942 in an effort to deliver important messages to the American public through advertisement. Topics of Ad Council PSAs include education, environmental protection, prevention of forest fires, drunk driving, and crime. The organization's Web site provides information about current and previous campaigns, as well as facts about their impact.

Advertising Educational Foundation (AEF)

220 E. Forty-second St., Suite 3300
New York, NY 10017-5806
(212) 986-8060 • fax: (212) 986-8061
Web site: www.aef.com

AEF works, with support from the advertising industry, to promote a greater understanding of the role of advertising in both the economic and social spheres of society. Through the publication of the academic journal *Advertising and Society Review,* provision of classroom and professor resources, and sponsorship of conferences, the AEF encourages discussion and debate about the importance of advertising and its contributions to society. The AEF Good, Bad & Ugly Awards celebrate positive portrayals of women in advertising while pointing out and discouraging the negative portrayals. Information about educational programs and awards is available on the AEF Web site.

American Advertising Federation (AAF)

1101 Vermont Ave. NW, Suite 500, Washington, DC   20005
(202) 898-0089 • fax: (202) 898-0159
e-mail: aaf@aaf.org
Web site: www.aaf.org

AAF is a trade organization for corporations and individuals within the advertising industry. The AAF works to ensure that the advertising industry flourishes by providing individuals within the field the opportunity to collaborate and stay at the forefront of the latest advertising trends. Additionally, the organization encourages diversity within the industry through recognition of excellence in advertisements and workforce diversity.

Campaign for Tobacco-Free Kids

1400 Eye St. NW, Suite 1200, Washington, DC   20005
(202) 296-5469 • fax: (202) 296-5427
e-mail: info@tobaccofreekids.org
Web site: www.tobaccofreekids.org

The Campaign for Tobacco-Free Kids is dedicated to curbing tobacco use, and as a result reducing the number of related deaths. The campaign works not only to help smokers quit, but also to decrease the amount of harmful secondhand smoke that reaches nonsmokers. The organization fights to raise awareness about the marketing of tobacco products to children. Through educational materials and reports available on its Web site, individuals can learn more about the ways in which tobacco companies target youth with their advertisements and the failure of the cigarette companies' youth access initiatives.

Center for Media Literacy (CML)

23852 Pacific Coast Hwy. #472, Malibu, CA   90265
(310) 456-1225 • fax: (310) 456-0020
e-mail: cml@medialit.org
Web site: www.medialit.org

CML has been leading efforts to encourage media literacy since 1977 with the publication of the magazine *Media & Values*. Though the magazine ceased publication in 1993, CML continues to promote the need for critical thinking in relation to media issues through projects such as the MediaLit Kit, available on its Web site, that provides strategies for teaching individuals how to become more media savvy. Additionally, the organization's online reading room offers a searchable database of articles on topics such as advertising and consumerism, stereotyping and representation, and violence in the media.

Children's Market Services, Inc. (CMS)
1385 York Ave., New York, NY   10021
(212) 794-0983 • fax: (212) 396-1280
e-mail: trends2000@aol.com
Web site: www.kidtrends.com

CMS is a marketing research firm that works to provide companies with information about what trends and products interest children and teens. Through market planning, focus groups, and surveys, CMS produces annual reports and studies predicting what products will be most successful with American youth. The company also publishes two newsletters: *Kidstrends* and *Targeting Teens*, with subscriptions available on its Web site.

Commercial Alert
PO Box 19002, Washington, DC   20036
(202) 387-8030 • fax: (202) 234-5176
Web site: www.commercialalert.org

Commercial Alert is a nonprofit organization dedicated to ensuring that advertising does not infringe on the rights of individuals. One major focus of the organization is researching and analyzing the effect of advertising on children and young people. Commercial Alert's Web site has information about current campaigns tackling issues such as advertisements on the Public Broadcasting Service and commercialization in schools, along with information on how individuals can become involved in these initiatives. Articles on current advertising-related debates are also provided.

Media Awareness Network (MNet)
1500 Merivale Rd., 3rd Fl.
Ottawa, Ontario K2E 6Z5 Canada
(613) 224-7721 • fax: (613) 224-1958
e-mail: info@media-awareness.ca
Web site: www.media-awareness.ca

Beginning with its incorporation in 1996, MNet has worked to increase public understanding of the media and their approaches to news, entertainment, and commerce. MNet promotes critical evaluation of the messages presented by the media and offers educational materials, for both adults and young people, that provide information and strategies to create a more media literate public. The MNet Web site offers access to a searchable database of articles, research reports, and lesson plans on media issues such as advertising, violence, and stereotyping.

Media Education Foundation (MEF)
60 Masonic St., Northampton, MA   01060
(800) 897-0089 • fax: (800) 659-6882
e-mail: info@mediaed.org
Web site: www.mediaed.org

MEF produces documentaries and other educational materials concerning the negative impact of the media on society and democracy. The organization encourages individuals to critically examine and question the messages of advertisements, pop culture, and news organizations. MEF's Web site provides access to free study guides as well as links to other sites organized by topic.

National Advertising Review Council (NARC)
70 W. Thirty-sixth St., 13th Fl., New York, NY   10018

toll-free: (866) 334-6272
Web site: www.narcpartners.org

NARC promotes truth and accuracy in advertising through self-regulation by the advertising industry. The council encourages advertising companies to evaluate the information and messages being sent by the ads they produce in an effort to limit government involvement and regulation. Programs such as the Children's Advertising Review Unit focus on advertisements directed at young audiences. A link to this program's Web site and general information about self-regulatory programs can be found on NARC's Web site.

National Institute on Media and the Family
606 Twenty-fourth Ave. South, Suite 606
Minneapolis, MN   55454
(612) 672-5437 • fax: (612) 672-4113
Web site: www.mediafamily.org

The National Institute on Media and the Family is dedicated to researching the effect of media on youth in America, then providing educational information and advocating for change when needed. The institute does not seek censorship of the media but is concerned about the potentially harmful consequences related to the consumption of certain types of media by impressionable youth. *Mediawise,* the newsletter of the institute is available online, as are fact sheets on topics such as the effect of advertising on children.

New Mexico Media Literacy Project (NMMLP)
6400 Wyoming Blvd. NE, Albuquerque, NM   87109
(505) 828-3129 • fax: (505) 828-3142
e-mail: nmmlp@nmmlp.org
Web site: www.nmmlp.org

Since 1993, NMMLP has provided educational materials to schools and individuals in an effort to increase the public's ability to critically assess the messages of the media. The organization's Web site provides extensive information on how to become more media savvy, including basic concepts of media literacy as well as questions to ask of advertisers that can help consumers better decipher the hidden messages. NMMLP also encourages individuals to take an active role in the creation of responsible media with the Talk Back to Big Tobacco! Script and Storyboard Contest.

Nielsen Business Media
770 Broadway, New York, NY   10003-9595
(646) 654-4500
e-mail: bmcomm@nielsen.com
Web site: www.nielsenbusiness.com

As a division of the Nielsen Company, Nielsen Business Media works to provide businesses with insight into the expectations of their target markets. Through publications such as *Billboard* and the *Hollywood Reporter*, the company assesses and drives trends in the music and film industries, respectively. Nielsen Business Media also organizes yearly conferences such as *What Teens Want* to share information about what the youth of America look for in advertisements and brands.

Bibliography

Books

Daniel Acuff and
Robert Reiher

Kidnapped: How Irresponsible Marketers Are Stealing the Minds of Your Children. Chicago: Dearborn Trade, 2005.

Henry A. Giroux

Stealing Innocence: Corporate Culture's War on Children. New York: Palgrave, 2000.

Lynn R. Kahle
and Chris Riley,
eds.

Sports Marketing and the Psychology of Marketing Communication. Mahwah, NJ: Erlbaum, 2004.

Jean Kilbourne

Deadly Persuasion: Why Women and Girls Must Fight the Addictive Power of Advertising. Tampa, FL: Free Press, 1999.

Jean Kilbourne
and Mary Pipher

Can't Buy Me Love: How Advertising Changes the Way We Think and Feel. Tampa, FL: Free Press, 2000.

Jerry Kirkpatrick

In Defense of Advertising: Arguments from Reason, Ethical Egoism, and Laissez-Faire Capitalism. Claremont, CA: TLJ Books, 2007.

Sharon Lamb and
Lyn Mikel Brown

Packaging Girlhood: Rescuing Our Daughters from Marketers' Schemes. New York: St. Martin's, 2006.

Murray Milner Jr. *Freaks, Geeks, and Cool Kids: American Teenagers, Schools, and the Culture of Consumption.* New York: Routledge, 2004.

Alex Molnar *School Commercialism: From Democratic Ideal to Market Commodity.* New York: Routledge, 2005.

Alissa Quart *Branded: The Buying and Selling of Teenagers.* New York: Perseus, 2003.

Juliet B. Schor *Born to Buy: The Commercialized Child and the New Consumer Culture.* New York: Scribner, 2005.

David Siegel, Timothy Coffey, and Gregory Livingston *The Great Tween Buying Machine: Capturing Your Share of the Multi-Billion-Dollar Tween Market.* Chicago: Dearborn Trade, 2004.

Clete Snell *Peddling Poison: The Tobacco Industry and Kids.* Westport, CT: Praeger, 2005.

James Twitchell *Adcult USA.* New York: Columbia University Press, 1996.

Advertising Age James Twitchell *Twenty Ads That Shook the World: The Century's Most Groundbreaking Advertising and How It Changed Us All.* New York: Three Rivers, 2000.

Periodicals

Alcoholism & Drug Abuse Weekly	"Causal Link Shown Between Alcohol Ads and Increased Drinking in Young People," January 9, 2006.
Atlantic Monthly	"Reverse Psychology," March 2007.
Neal Broverman	"Keeping Youth Off Crystal," *Advocate*, July 5, 2005.
Brown University Child & Adolescent Behavior Letter	"Alcohol and Tobacco Marketing Targets Hispanic Youth," January 2006.
Dermatology Nursing	"Cancer Update: Campaign Sends Strong Message to Teens About Dangers of Indoor Tanning," February 2007.
Becky Ebenkamp and Sandra O'Loughlin	"Charlie Is a Hot Topic for Teens," *Brandweek*, August 22, 2005.
Gordon Fairclough	"Study Slams Philip Morris Ads Telling Teens Not to Smoke," *Wall Street Journal*, May 29, 2002.
Mya Frazier	"Wal-Mart Tries to Be MySpace. Yes, Seriously," *Advertising Age*, July 17, 2006.
Bob Garfield	"A Powerful Lesson That Will Surely Be Forgotten," *Advertising Age*, March 27, 2006.

Amy Gilroy "Teen Marketing Gets Reviewed at CES Seminar," *TWICE: This Week in Consumer Electronics*, January 24, 2005.

Stephanie Kang "All Wet? Retailer Calls in Teen 'Stylizers' to Revive Sales," *Wall Street Journal*, July 30, 2004.

Juli B. Kramer "Ethical Analysis and Recommended Action in Response to the Dangers Associated with Youth Consumerism," *Ethics and Behavior*, October 2006.

Alex Kuczynski "Teenage Magazines Mostly Reject Breast Enlargement Ads," *New York Times*, August 13, 2001.

Inmaculada Jose Martinez, Maria Dolores Prieto, and Juana Farfan "Childhood and Violence in Advertising: A Current Perspective," *International Communication Gazette*, June 2006.

Dave McCaughan "Teens Are Hung Up on Mobile," *Advertising Age*, January 22, 2007.

Jack Neff "The Real Axe Effect," *Advertising Age*, May 15, 2006.

Jack Neff "Zit Cream Targets Teens with Direct Web Effect," *Advertising Age*, May 7, 2007.

Jeff Niederdeppe, Matthew C. Farrelly, and Dana Wenter "Media Advocacy, Tobacco Control Policy Change and Teen Smoking in Florida," *Tobacco Control*, February 2007.

Sandra O'Loughlin	"Targeting Trendy Teens with Free T's," *Brandweek*, May 23, 2005.
Michael Paoletta	"Sprite Exposed," *Billboard*, July 8, 2006.
Sonia Reyes	"The Rap on Milk?" *Brandweek*, March 26, 2007.
J. Russell	"Target Demos: Moms, Youths," *Television Week*, September 12, 2005.
David Steinberger	"Isn't Getting Teens to Read a Good Thing?" *Publishers Weekly*, August 7, 2006.
Stephanie Thompson	"Coty Brings London to Teens via Makeup Line," *Advertising Age*, October 9, 2006.
Todd Wasserman	"Playing the Hip-Hop Name Drop," *Brandweek*, July 25, 2005.
Tina Wells	"What Teens Want," *Billboard*, October 20, 2006.
Lara Zwarun et al.	"Effects of Showing Risk in Beer Commercials to Young Drinkers," *Journal of Broadcasting & Electronic Media*, March 2006.

Index